THE OTHER BROTHER

WRITTEN BY

Melody Carlson

ILLUSTRATED BY

Steve Björkman

CROSSWAY BOOKS . WHEATON, ILLINOIS

A DIVISION OF GOOD NEWS PUBLISHERS

The Other Brother

Text copyright © 1999 by Melody Carlson

Illustration copyright © 1999 by Steve Björkman

Design by Cindy Kiple

Published by Crossway Books
a division of Good News Publishers
1300 Crescent Street
Wheaton, Illinois 60187

First printing, 1999

Printed in the United States of America

LIBRARY OF CONGRESS CATALOGING-IN-PUBLICATION DATA

Carlson, Melody.
    The other brother / written by Melody Carlson : illustrated by Steve Björkman.
       p.   cm.
    Summary: A contemporary retelling, in rhyming text, of the parable of the prodigal son.
    ISBN 1-58134-122-9 (alk. paper)
    1. Prodigal son (Parable) Juvenile literature. [1. Prodigal son (Parable) 2. Parables 3. Bible stories--N.T.] I. Björkman, Steve, ill. II. Bible N.T. Luke XV, 11-32. English. 1999. III. Title.
BT378.P8C27 1999
226.8'09505--dc21

                                                  99-16674
                                                  CIP

08	07	06	05	04	03	02	01	00	99
15	14	13	12	11	10	9	8	7	6	5	4	3	2	1

To the "other brothers" —

Gabe and Luke—

May your friendship continue to grow.

All my love,

Mom

For Gordon Stromberg—

The right man at the right time.

Thanks,

Steve

There was a man who had two boys.

His only sons—his pride and joy!

He hoped one day they'd run his farm,

And keep the animals safe from harm.

The first son's name was Malachi.

Hardworking boy, though kind of shy,

He was the best to rope and ride.

He liked to stand by his pop's side.

The second son was Benjamin.

He was tall and kind of thin.

He loved to spend his spare time fishing,

Dreaming dreams and always wishing.

Ben said to Pops, "I need some money.

I need to go where it is sunny."

He packed his things and waved good-bye

To his dear Pops and Malachi.

Ben spent his cash on a big boat

And went to sea, his boat to float.

At last, at last, he got his wish—

Now all day long, he'd fish for fish!

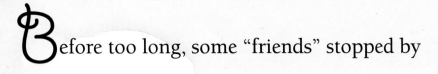Before too long, some "friends" stopped by

To give his boat a little try…

They greeted Ben, all hale and hearty,

And said, "Let's throw a floating party!"

They rocked and rolled upon the sea.

They laughed and joked and watched TV.

They ate his food and drank his drink,

And then Ben's boat began to sink!

$\mathcal{H}$is friends got mad and went away.

Without a boat, not one would stay.

Ben said, "You guys, this isn't funny.

My boat is sunk—I'm out of money!"

Poor Ben was broke—now he was stuck,

Out of friends and out of luck.

He got a job with Farmer Boggs.

He cleaned the barn and fed the hogs.

The pay was poor, and Ben worked hard.

What he would give for beans 'n' lard.

He worked from dawn till dark of dusk.

He was so starved he ate corn husks.

One day while Ben ate with the hogs,

He said, "This life is for the dogs!

Workin' for Pops was better than this."

He thought of all the things he missed.

And so Ben told old Boggs good-bye.

He would go home, his luck to try.

He hoped his pops would take him in

To feed the pigs and clean their pen.

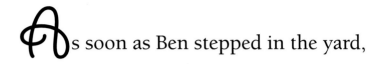

As soon as Ben stepped in the yard,

He knew this meeting would be hard.

He sobbed and fell onto his knees.

"Forgive me, Pops—I beg you, please!"

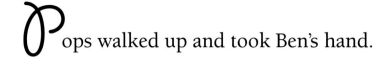ops walked up and took Ben's hand.

He hugged him tight and helped him stand.

"When you left, I thought you'd died.

Welcome home, my son!" Pops cried.

ops gave to Ben the very best

Of cowboy boots and leather vest.

He said, "Dear Ben, how I missed you.

Now we shall have a bar-b-cue!"

Against the fence leaned Malachi,

A jealous look was in his eye.

"It's just not fair," he said to Pops.

"Ben blew it bad, and now he's tops!"

$\mathcal{P}$ops said, "My son, now don't you see

What's mine is yours—you stayed with me!

When Ben left home we feared him dead.

Now he's back—let's rejoice instead."

LUKE 15:11-32

A certain man had two sons…
The younger one took his inheritance and went far away…
And there he wasted his money on a wasteful lifestyle…
And soon he became very poor…
And he was sent to feed the pigs…
And he would gladly have eaten the pigs' food…
For nobody gave him anything.

But when he came to his senses, he said,
"My father's servants have food to spare
And here I am dying of hunger.
I will go home and apologize,
And ask to be like a servant."

When his father saw him, he ran and kissed him.
And the son said, "Father, I have sinned against you
And I'm not worthy to be called your son."
But the father said, "Bring out my best robe,
And kill the fatted calf. For my son who was dead is alive."

But the older son was angry and wouldn't join the celebration.
So the father said to him, "Son, you've been with me always.
All I have is yours. It is right that we rejoice over your brother.
He once was lost and now is found. He was dead and is alive again!"

Paraphrased by the Author

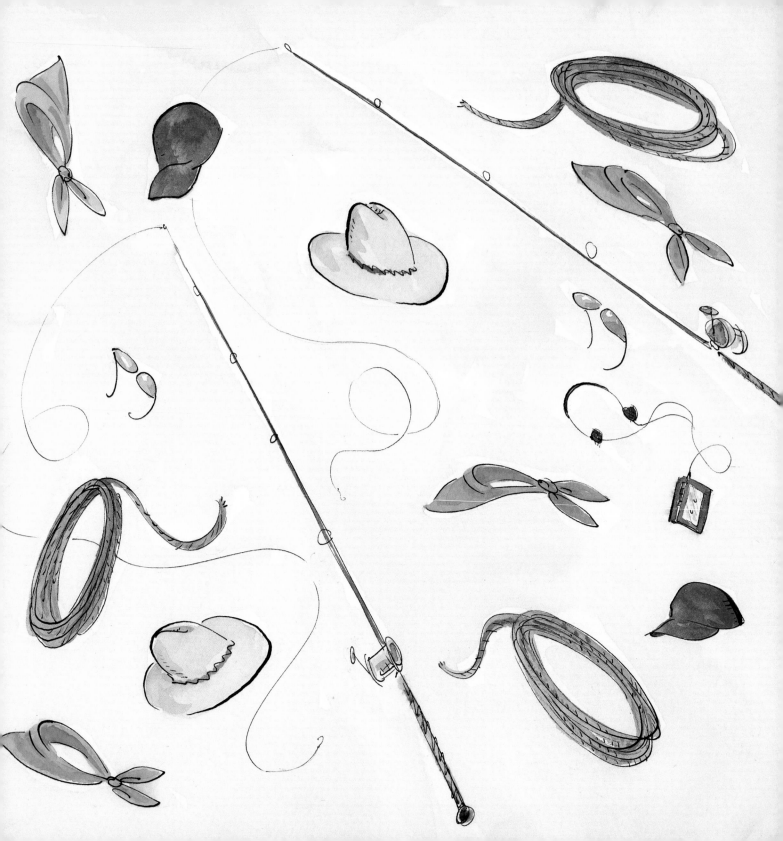